THE COLOUR OF THE WEATHER

THE COLOUR
OF THE WEATHER

an introduction to Belgian dialect poetry
selected and translated by

YANN LOVELOCK

THE MENARD PRESS
1980

THE COLOUR OF THE WEATHER

Anthology of Walloon poetry
Selection and editorial material and translations
©1979 Yann Lovelock

Original poems ©1979 (on behalf of the authors) Yann Lovelock
details of the provenance of the original poems,
those published in this selection and those not,
can be found in the biographical notes

Cover illustration is by Jean Donnay

The Menard Press here acknowledges its 1979–80 grant from
the Arts Council of Great Britain

ISBN (hardback) 0 903400 47 2
ISBN (paperback) 0 903400 48 0

The Menard Press is a member of ALP

Menard Press books are distributed in the USA and Canada by
SBD: Small Press Distribution, 1636 Ocean View Avenue,
Kensington California 94707

THE MENARD PRESS
23 Fitzwarren Gardens
London N19 3TR

Printed in England by
Skelton's Press Limited, Wellingborough, Northamptonshire.

Acknowledgements

I wish to thank all those poets who gave permission for their work to appear in this anthology, and particularly those who sent me scripts and helped me with their interpretation. Among these, I owe a particular debt to Willy Bal, Emile Lempereur, Charles Geerts, Albert Yande and Jean Guillaume, who helped me with further information, biographical, bibliographical, on subjects relative to the dialect, and in obtaining material. In addition, I would like to thank Henri Prémont for putting me in touch with some of the poets who appear here. I would also like to remember Milton Rosenthal, formerly of UNESCO's Literature Division, who sent me Maurice Piron's *Poètes Wallons d'aujourd'hui*, the anthology which first aroused my interest in this field, and whose colleagues especially Lionel Izod have been kind enough to help with the publication of the present anthology.

Acknowledgements are due to the following magazines in which some of these translations first appeared: *Broadsheet* (Eire); *El Mouchon d'Aunia* (Belgium); *Iron; Urbane Gorilla; Joe Soap's Canoe; Pennine Platform; Trends.*

UNESCO COLLECTION
OF REPRESENTATIVE WORKS
EUROPEAN SERIES

This book has been accepted in the European Series of the
Translations Collection of the United Nations Educational,
Scientific and Cultural Organization (Unesco)

Contents

Introduction   9
Gabrielle Bernard   21
Géo Libbrecht   22
Charles Geerts   24
Henri Collette   26
René Painblanc   27
Franz Dewandelaer   28
Max-André Frère   31
Albert Yande   32
Emile Lempereur   34
Louis Remacle   35
Jeanne Houbart-Houge   37
Willy Bal   39
Marcel Hicter   41
Jean Guillaume   43
Léon Warnant   45
Josée Spinosa-Mathot   47
Albert Maquet   48
Marc Deburges   51
Jules Flabat   52
Nicholas Donnay   53
Jenny d'Inverno   54
Emile Gilliard   55
Georges Smal   56
Biographical Notes   59
Further Reading   63
Note on Editor Translator   63

Introduction

A dialect, as distinguished from regional mannerisms and acents on the one hand, and different but associated languages on the other, might be described as differing from the 'metropolitan' language of which it is a variant not only in pronunciation, but in possessing significant peculiarities of syntax and a wide range of alternative vocabulary. Another characteristic is that a dialect differs from region to region, a result of its popular character outside of the standardising processes of the official language. In the various parts of south-eastern Belgium where the Walloon dialects are spoken, for example, the word for sun (*le soleil* in standard French) is variously expressed as *l'solèy, l'sèlo, l'sulo, li solo, lë solia, el soya*.

Although literature in Walloon can claim a history of some three and a half centuries, it is only during the last hundred years or so that a self-conscious effort has been made to create a substantial written literature in the popular idiom. That it had remained for so long an oral means of communication meant at first that there was no standard orthography. Authors spelt by ear and according to their personal idiosyncrasies. Recent scholarship has done much to put this right, especially in the province of Liège, and there is a stricter attention to the vocabulary. French words which have crept into the dialect are excluded when there is a valid Walloon expression to take its place. There are now evening classes devoted to the study of the dialect and it has even found its way onto the school curriculum; there is great enthusiasm for this in Liège and the southern part of Brabant, but in Hainaut the teaching profession is divided and an element of snobbery plays its part in the issue.

It is not surprising that in a country with the troubled linguistic inheritance of Belgium the inhabitants should be given to linguistic self-consciousness or that the authorities should be sympathetic to it. To the north and west Flemish dialects are spoken, but as a reaction to the francophone dominance that obtained after the creation of the country in 1830, and for the sake of solidarity, Dutch has been adopted as the language of education and literature in these areas. In parts of Luxembourg province adjoining the Grand Duchy there are still some speakers of the latter's German Letzburgesch dialect, and related Middle-German dialects are spoken by many about St Vith and other districts to the east of Liège province in the areas annexed from Germany in 1918. French, for long the official language of Belgium, is now officially confined to the south-eastern provinces of Hainaut, Namur, southern Brabant, Liège and Luxembourg.

It is in these that the dialects occur. The term 'Walloon' is sometimes used to cover all of them, but strictly speaking there are three, more or less continguous. That of Gaume (*le gaumais*) in the west is confined to the south of Luxembourg province, while to the east Picard is spoken in the greater part of Hainaut province as far as a line drawn between Braine le Compte and Binche. It also crosses the frontier into France, where it is spoken in those parts annexed from the ancient county of Hainaut (capital, Valenciennes), and in the province of Picardy as far south as Beauvais and Senlis. Western Walloon is spoken in the rest of Hainaut, central dialects in Namur and eastern in Liège. Theoretically all are mututally intelligible, but in practice this is not always so. One can talk of their morphology only in very general terms. Thus, for example –

1) Latin initial *c* before *a* remains as such in Picard but becomes *tch* in Walloon: Latin *cantare*, French *chanter*, Picard *canter*, Walloon *tchanter*.

2) Latin initial *g* before *a* remains as such in Picard but becomes *dj* in Walloon: Low Lat. *gamba*, Fr. *jambe*, Pic. *gambe*, Wall. *djambe*.

3) Latin *c* before *e* or *i* becomes *ch* in Picard and *s* (ordinarily written *c*) in Walloon: Lat. *cinerem*, Fr. *cendre*, Pic. *chinde* or *chène*, Wall. *cinde*.

4) Latin termination *-ellum* becomes *-iau* in Picard, *-ia* in western and central Walloon, *-ê* in eastern dialect. Low Lat. *capellum*, Fr. *chapeau*, Pic. *capiau*, W. and Cent. Wall. *tchapia*, E. Wall. *tchapê*.

5) Latin medial *s* before most unvoiced consonants is generally lost in Picard but retained in Walloon: Lat. *castellum*, Fr. *château*, Pic. *catyeau*, E. Wall. *tchêstê*.

How complicated the linguistic map can be in Hainaut may be gathered from the following extract from a book on the province. 'Between the Picard and Walloon areas there is a transitional zone in which dialectal characteristics are jumbled. The word for hat in the Soignies/ La Louvière regions is *capia*, with a Picard beginning and a Walloon termination. But round about Rance and Chimay they say *tchapiau*, a Walloon beginning with Picard termination! Another example of complexity is that the indubitably Picard dialect of the Tournai area is far from homogenous: it is possible to distinguish the town dialect, the 'pladeau' of the left-hand bank of the Escaut, and the 'hainuy' of the right. The Borinage dialect is uniform only to those from outside the area: where they say *chinde, glache, martiau* (Fr. *cendre, glace, marteau*) at Pâturages, Wasmes and Quaregnon, it's *cinde, glace, martia* at Frameries. A fine subject of reflection for the partisans of dialect studies in school!'[1]

What Albert Yande has to say on the subject of dialect in notes he sent me relevant to his work holds true for all: 'Dialects or popular idioms are losing ground from generation to generation and in any case are becoming less and less pure since young people no longer get to learn them at home. They are adulterated more and more with words of French origin which are given a dialectal semblance in pronunciation. In reaction, intellectual and university circles have tended to create literary movements whose aim is to produce and above all augment the patrimony of dialectal literature by the production and diffusion of written works, plays and songs equally valuable from the literary as from the dialectal points of view. More and more notice is taken of the traditional particularities of the spoken idiom and of the folklore of the people in order to preserve their uniqueness in the economic and political conglomerations various European countries are setting up to unify them while neglecting perhaps too often and too much the human aspect.'

There is something of the imperialist and bully about metropolitan culture. Belgium has often suffered by having her best writers lured to Paris (as London once lured the Scots and Irish) or, like Verhaeren for example, annexed in spite of her. Snobbery plays its part as well. Speakers of other languages and dialects are made to feel inferior and must submit to hearing their idioms described officially as 'a mere patois'. Reactions can be extreme: some would claim for Walloon, with its Celtic and Germanic admixtures, the status of a language since it derives (in common with the others) directly from the Low Latin rather than the corruption of French, which the official view would falsely make it out to be. Charles Geerts recalls that his grandmother was unable to converse in anything but Walloon. Nowadays,, what with its shrinkage going hand in hand with the growth of the mass media, a writer such as René Painblanc admits to reading and speaking as little as possible in French in order to conserve the purity of his Walloon thought and expression.

Even if there are few, if any, Walloon monoglots now, the dialect survives. Naturally the greater part of its speakers are of lower class and rural origin, but not all. It acts as a link between people from the same district now living or working elsewhere, and they will drop into the popular idiom when talking among themselves. Over the years the number writing in Walloon, often turning to it in middle or old age, has been steadily growing, and this too has acted as a stimulus. Belgian radio and television devotes some of its time (and that at peak hours as well) to dialect productions, especially in the traditionally popular field of sketches, domestic comedy and drama. Chekhov, Molière and Shakespeare are among those whose work has been adapted into Walloon.

A great deal of energy, by no means all of it deriving from literary quarters, has gone towards creating the climate in which this literature has been enabled to burgeon. Of primary importance was the institution of the biennial prize for Walloon literature at Liège in 1925, the money for which was raised by public subscription in two years of hectic agitation, although in 1931 the town took over this lump sum and guaranteed the prize for the future. Works of lyrical poetry gain the preference although prose and drama are not overlooked. The prize has something of the cachet of the Prix Goncourt, with the Prix des Critiques Wallons, established in 1951, taking second place. There are now numerous other prizes, both provincial and national.

Associated with or awarding these are a number of associations and groups, of which the most important are the national Association des écrivains dialectaux et francophones and La Société de langue et de littérature wallonnes, known as the 'dialectal academy'. Among the chief regional groups are Hainaut's Scrîveûs du Cente, Les Rèlîs Namurwès, Les auteurs wallons liègois, and the Groupement des auteurs dialectaux luxembourgeois of which Albert Yande is president. These in turn have their magazines which are widely read beyond the nucleus of their membership: the bulletins of the SLLW and AWL, for example, or Charles Geerts' *Mouchon d'Aunia* which has now been in existence for 66 years. These and other dialect publications, beside translations, prose, verse and drama, cover criticism, local history, folklore and the remains of oral literature, etymology, and so on. Several, other examples are *La Vie Wallonne* (Liège), *El Bourdon* (Charleroi), *Cahiers Wallons* (Namur), devote an issue to the work of one poet or turn their presses to the production of booklets as well. Other poets, less fortunate, use their prize money to have a book printed, often with French translations opposite or a comprehensive word-list.

Much of any dialect poetry tends to be, though charming, of trifling content and significance. That Walloon poetry has transcended these limitations is largely due to its becoming a tool of the educated at the moment of the spoken idiom's retreat before education. One might compare its flourishing in this century to what has taken place in Lallans (Scots) poetry thanks to the efforts of Hugh MacDiarmid and those who followed him in Scotland. Some of the foremost 19th century writers in Walloon were self-taught men and affected such 'literary' forms as the sonnet and rondel. Nor are such given up even now, and there are still *autodidactes* such as René Painblanc and Josée Spinosa-Mathot to carry on the popular tradition, not to mention deliberate primitives like Willy Bal and Emile Gilliard. Besides those writing with colloquial energy – and here one would add the distinctive voice of Franz Dewandelaer to those of Painblanc and Bal – and others whose style might be described as mainstream, one must distinguish those academics and others who seem to have drawn their inspiration from the Belgian Symbolists (with a dash of surrealism here and there) to create works of great sophistication and beauty.

That Symbolist echoes should be so prevalent in modern verse may be the result both of atavism and education. The poets who made up the Jeune Belgique movement of the 1880's, although subscribing to French Symbolist or Parnassian theory, nevertheless created a national poetry for the first time, the achievements of which have never

quite been equalled since. Not all their traits and pre-
occupations have been taken over into Walloon writing.
There is none of the satanic decadence of an Iwan Gilkin or
Albert Giraud, such as is to be found in the English
Symbolists of the last century. Nor of the Flemish robustness
which Verhaeren recorded with such exuberance in his
early verse that it earned him the title of 'the Raphael of
filth' from one disapproving reviewer. Again, there is not
much, if anything, of his grudging celebration of the pro-
ducts of industrialism – the 'tentacular town' to which all
roads lead – in his later verse.

It is, rather, the Verhaeren of the neurasthenic poems
written during his nervous crisis, and of the countryside,
who seems to have impressed the Walloons and found an
echo in their heart. Jenny d'Inverno's coalescing of emo-
tional and seasonal weathers in 'Weather's Colour' surely
stems from poems like Verhaeren's 'Fogs':

> You melancholy fogs of winter roll
> Your pestilential sorrow o'er my soul,
> And swathe my heart with your long winding-sheet,
> And drench the livid leaves beneath my feet,
> While far away upon the heaven's bounds,
> Under the plain's wet wadding, sounds
> A tired, lamenting angelus that dies
> With faint, frail echoes in the empty skies,
> So lonely, poor and timid that a rook,
> Hid in a hollow archstone's dripping nook,
> Hearing it sob, awakens and replies,
> Sickening the woeful hush with ghastly cries,
> Then suddenly grows silent, in the dread
> That in the belfry tower the bell is dead.[2]

There are also in Jean Guillaume numerous echoes of
Verhaeren, but he is an academic who specialises in the
period.

Though it is hard to find parallels for the extremes of
debilitated melancholia which is the master-theme of

Maeterlinck's verse, there is a good deal of gentler melancholy and of regret, especially for the lost moments of carefree happiness in youth. It is instructive here to compare Remacle's handling of such themes with the young Dewandelaer's vigorous recreation of his boyhood or the wry serenity of Geerts' old age. Such themes in the hands of Lempereur, Remacle and others seem to have their starting-point in the poetry of Grégoire le Roy. One might cite, among many examples, the 'Roundel of old women' which begins

Little old women, my thoughts,
The snow falls from the vast,
Death and uncertainty palls
All the things of the past.

Why is my heart so chill
Under these skies overcast,
In these winters that last and last,
These winters calm and still?

You little old women who glean,
Make a bonfire of your past,
Of your reeds snapped by the blast,
And of all your barren dreams.

All that your sorrow remembers,
Burn it like dry brushwood,
And sit and warm your blood
Over the dying embers.

Perhaps it is to Le Roy that we should go for a clarification of Maquet's mysterious 'What time is left' in the light of the grand guignol of the former's 'Hands', especially the opening verses:

Glued like the eyes of a thief
At my heart's windowpane, gazing in,
Were two pale hands, hands of grief,
Hands as of Death, bone and skin.

I shivered to see them stare,
Weird as the moon in the blue,
Lifting to me their despair,
As the hands of the damned might do.

And He of those desolate hands,
Who was my visitor grim?
Death on my threshold stands,
Since I gazed on the hands of Him.

One of the main Symbolist techniques was to suggest meanings by the creation of an atmosphere within the poem without making any outright statement, or by a concentrated treatment of an object really symbolic of the poem's underlying theme. As a well-known French statement of the Symbolist aim puts it, 'évoquer petit à petit un objet pour montrer un état d'âme, ou inversement choisir un objet et en dégager un état d'âme'. The delicate art of Charles van Lerberghe was admirably suited to this. The gradual merging of natural elements into personal symbols, which we find in Smal or Gabrielle Bernard, for example, has its genesis in a poem like the following:

How many blond hours
held in the golden grape
of this world's-morning
where my light sleeps!

They are eternal,
the briefest of them
in my joyous summer
worth an eternity.

Look at me as I bend
my dream above your eyes:
fruit and leaf, the bough
is mingled with your hair.

Sing, and remember
your first ray of light;
you hardly see me,
but I shine on your brow.[3]

Ageing and death is a common preoccupation of both sets of writers; even allowing for its being a perennial theme in all poetry, it cannot escape a reader's notice how obsessional a subject it has become among the Walloons. Death of the spirit as a result of the inturning caused by crushing hardship appears more rarely in the work of the Symbolists. Few besides Verhaeren treated it on so realistic a level, as in his 'The Fishermen' or the equally sombre early poem, 'Peasants'. The latter is both defence of and diatribe against rustic meanness and its attendant squalor. Conditions are appalling,

> So like an ulcer hate is in their hearts,
> Patient and cunning hate with smiling face.
> Their frank and loud good humour hatches rage;
> Wickedness glimmers in their icy looks.
> They stink of the rancorous gall that, age by age,
> Their sufferings have collected in their souls.
> Keen are they on the slightest gain, and mean;
> Since they can not enrich themselves by work,
> Stinginess makes their hearts hard, their hearts fetid;
> And black their mind is, set on petty things,
> And stupid and confounded before great . . . .
> And when Death opens unto them its doors,
> Their coffin sliding into the soft earth
> Seems only to contain a thing twice dead.

Such a theme is returned to time and again by the Walloons – Lempereur, Guillaume, Bal, Donnay and many others – and forms the basis of their social criticism.

If a charge of conservatism were to be brought against these writers, as it must in the case of several, it should not be simply because they have been so indebted to Symbolism. In that the literary movement marked the beginning of modernism in European literature, we should be surprised at its absence. Of writing in our own country John Press remarks that 'the past fifty years have witnessed the attempts of our most gifted poets to incorporate the heritage of Symbolism into the structure of their verse, to express the concepts of a European aesthetic revolution'[4]. A glance at the state of the game today might suggest we have succeeded less well than the Walloons.

Where they might be faulted is in their tending to concentrate to a great extent on the melancholy and rural aspects of life to the exclusion of other interests, such as those of Verhaeren already mentioned, and this in one of the most highly industrialised countries in Europe. Here it is possible that the language they use betrays them in part. The dialect was bred and persists among country communities whose interest and outlook it serves. Where it differs most from metropolitan speech is precisely in expressing these areas. But there are benefits also, for wedded to the advanced style and approach of the moderns is a poetry of great chastity, lacking those 'literary' elements, either luscious or arid, which are often the mark of poetry written in standard French. Nor must it be imagined that Walloon writers have turned their backs altogether on what is happening in the world around them. I am only too aware that it may be a quirk of my own taste that leads me to prefer those poems most reminiscent of a past era. That so much is to be found in a period spanning fifty years, however, suggests that I have not wholly misrepresented what is, at the least, a major characteristic of Walloon writing.

YANN LOVELOCK

Birmingham, August 1974–*November* 1979

NOTES

[1] See *Le Hainaut* in the La Belgique des Régions series, Editions Labor, 1977. Much of the preceding dialectal information is drawn from the same source.

[2] Translated by Jethro Bithell in his anthology *Contemporary Belgian Poets* in the Canterbury Poets series (Walter Scott, London, 1911), from which the other poems by Verhaeren and Le Roy are taken.

[3] For the French text, see *The Penguin Book of French Verse 4: the* 20*th century.*

[4] John Press, *The Fire and the Fountain* (2nd ed., Methuen, London, 1966), p.96.

GABRIELLE BERNARD

Cobwebs

Their skeins stretch
like white silk between the hedges
as October rusts the woods.

Mornings grow cooler,
frost whitens the pastures.

Gossamer down flume-sides
webbed by the dew with pearls . . .

The north wind whispers a winter warning.

Is it white mourning for the bright summer,
this gossamer everywhere,
spun from witches' fingers over beck and dyke?

Roadside gossamer;
dreams of cold days to come;
the farms have gathered in the harvest.

Slopes of gossamer . . .

Webs on the bushes,
white shivering weeds of the good season,
trembling on leaves already withered . . .

Gossamered temples . . .
what use is plenty in the barns
when heart and arms are empty?

Cha ch'est famile

Bé, te coneos bon ceul' famile
qu'èle a d'meuré au fourbou d'Lille
in fac' du molumint Noté
d'ùs que l'gramère a décédé
d'bwar sés p'tit chinot in cachète:
ch'éteot èn bèon gross badoulète
mêm' qu'el aveot in faux chigneon,
in orgard d'carcayeot mareon
ét dés déchirurt' à s'cotreon.
L'grand-pèr' ch'teot in fouteû d'cacoules,
in albran de l'pu pire andoule,
i-ést intyéré com' balotil
més cha n'éteot qu'in agozil.
T'as conu s'mère in grant twalète
qu'èle éteot toudi in couchète,
ét l'mopère el grand cachiveû
qui-aveot pou métyér d'èt' wieû.
Pour èn famil' cha ch'ést famile:
lés seiz fèss' fézeotte syèt files
ét lés deux restant el garchéon
qui a fét deux treos meos d'prisèon
au Catyeau Spreux dés chint mill' briques
pour avoir volé à s'fabrique;
au feond cha n'éteot qu'in mouklyeû,
in vré p'tit sèrpint imblémeû,
i s'a maryé avèc èn rousse,
el fil' de l'fèm de l'*Vak qui tousse*
qu'on n'a jamé vu qu'pieds dékéaus
tout épouti d'dins s'carakeo:
à l'époqu' de l'talidumite,
on dit – més ch'n'ést po mi qui l'dit
ét si te l'répèt ch'ést tanpis –
qu'èle a mis au mèonte in gamin
arnaké d'èn tyète ed Flamind.

GÉO LIBBRECHT

There's a family

Here, you know that family
lived up the Faubourg de Lille
on the other side from the statue
where the grandmother died
of taking a nip on the sly:
she was a good, fat soul
even if she did have false hair,
a face like a fish
and rips in her apron . . . .
The grandad was a humbug, though,
a good-for-nothing of the worst,
and it served him right
he got buried like he did.
You knew how the mother dolled up
never out of her dressing-gown,
and that bleary-eyed father of theirs
made being a lazybones his living.
Well, there's a family for you:
eight fat arses of kids,
seven girls, and a boy
did two or three months behind bars
in that brick-heap they call Spreux Castle
for stealing from his factory –
all gas and no go, he was,
the poison little serpent,
and married that redhead
whose mother runs the Coughing Cow
and you never saw anything but barefoot
with a housecoat wrapped around her;
that time they raved over shrimps of girls,
it's said . . . . but I haven't told you, mind,
it'd be too bad if you were to spread it,
she brought a brat into this world
had a head on him like a Fleming's.

Tant qu'à s'cousin, ceul' grant rambile
i-a mal tourné, i-ést garde-vile,
èt tout l'rèste i ést à l'av'nint:
pour èn famil' cha ch'ést famile!

Picard dialect of Tournai

CHARLES GEERTS

Boulomes

Padrî mi du vwas des-anéyes
assèz pou d-in fé dîs romans
ène 'sinfonîye' inachèvéye
mîse à l'ascoute su l'ér du tamps.
    Mètnant,mi,dèpassè,vî ome,
    du cache su l'tchèmin des-èfants
    in crèyon pou fé des boulomes ...

Padrî mi du vwas des ducaces
des valseûs dins l'souyin spardu
èyè des coupes gagnî-n leû place
in s'inspètant Dieù sét ayu.
    Mètnant,mi,intrè deûs ptits somes
    du cache dins des-autès sadjus
    in crèyon pou fé des boulomes ...

Padrî mi du vwas n'ribambène
d'ancyins djon.nes spliquant leûs souvnis
tant èt pus dusqu'à djus d'alène
à leû môde èt sans trop minti.
    Pusquè du sûs dèvnu vî-ome
    qu'i pluvisse ou bî-n qu'i fzisse bon
    avû l'èfant dè no méson
    pa plési ... du fés des boulomes.

Dialect of Morlanwelz, E. Hainaut province

As for their cousin, the young limb,
he turned out wrong, he joined the police,
and all the rest are just as bad.
Now there's a family for you.

CHARLES GEERTS

Matchstick men

(FOR MY GRANDDAUGHTER, NADIA GEERTS)

I can look back on years enough
to fill a dozen story books,
an uncompleted symphony
broadcast over the air of time . . . .
    Outdistanced, grown an old man now,
    I look down childhood's highway for
    a pencil to make matchstick men.

I can look back on kermess fairs,
the bandstands with the waltzers round
and couples leaving one by one
to hide out God alone knows where.
    Now I, between two little naps,
    look in quite other places for
    a pencil to make matchstick men.

Follow my leader, I look back
on young men old with memories
to give them talk till breath runs out
without embroidering too much.
    But rain or shine, since I've grown old,
    I can enjoy myself at home
    with a child making matchstick men.

HENRI COLLETTE

Dionysos*

I almost lost heart as I went back in.
'Lor, did you ever?' they bleat from the kitchen;
I peer at the mirror, my nose all yellow,
A dram the worse for the perfume of catkins.

Lugged home a fat knotted stick in one fist,
My hat in the other, ribboned with clover –
No saying the damage bushes have done it;
There's a button gone from my Sunday-best.

A splutter of heat! Spring's got his pipe alight
And puffs a great steaming cloud of vapour
Out of the greening woods in which he's shrouded.

My body this moment's worth more than fine clothes.
Life bursting at the seams, blood half-seas-over,
Pelican-like, I could rip myself open.

*The god of spring-tide renewal . . . and of drunkenness.
                    (Author's note)

RENE PAINBLANC

Four discs

My neighbour's moved and given me a collection of old stuff,
well knowing my mania for never throwing away
what a money-grubbing junkman wouldn't bother even
to cast his eye over if he happened to run up against it.

I've sorted out the best to be found while scratching
through cushions of mould in a worm-eaten box,
– rusty nails, buttons, blunt knives, pendants –
thinking 'That'll do, I haven't been wasting my time'.

Then, scraping the wood, my nails raked out
four red-copper discs not worth a second thought
unless to an old-fashioned type who's never disowned
the things he keeps snug where time's lost its grip.

For some it might be a trifle, to me it's a nest-egg:
four obsolete discs, piggy-bank of memories,
verdigris-stained . . . . these three little farthings
nestling in the dust beside an old ha'penny piece.*

* Literally three *djigots* and a *sance*, popular names for coins
worth one and two centimes respectively, withdrawn from use
during World War I.

Nivèle, quand vos r'vènez dins mès-îs r'qué vo place,
Fét-à m'zure què d'vos vwè l'djoû s'dèsface,
Lès souv'nances èrvikont, s'ravigotont d'vant mi,
Come l'afeuwure qui danse au trèfond du fourni . . .
Djé r'vwè toute èm-vik'réye . . . gamin . . . pus d'bras què d'manche . . .
Mwins d'guèrzèles que d'picots . . . pus d'am'djoûs què d'dimanches,
Mwins d'solèy què d'guèrjas . . . mains mwins d'brèyou què d'jwè
Pusquè d'vos viyou djà voltî sans trop l'savwè . . .
Yèt dj'é crèchî, pèlmi-pèlmèle avè l'rascaye,
Dins lès-èrtayes dè m'temps, dj'astou'ne pètite èrtaye,
Mains dj'astou chèf dès pwèy dins lès pwèy dè m'culot,
Dj'wétou d'avwè leû coeur, d'èrtènu leûs bias mots,
Djè grimpiou d'ssus lès saus come asteure dèssus l'vîye,
Djè viyou pus voltî lès nids d'pièrots qu'lès fîyes,
Djè chakinou, djè m'èrmètou su l'même moumint,
Djè d'nou, sans balziner, coup d'pougn èyèt coup d'main,
Dj'astou grand coudreû d'pums, mindjeû d'pèkes, skeûjeû d'prones,
L'chagrin passout tout-oute avè m'cu pa m'marone,
Mès cousses avin dè l'ér, mès poches aviń dès tròs,
Dj'astou minîr pou l'coeur, mains ni pou lès djigots . . . .

Dialect of Nivelles, S. Brabant province

FRANZ DEWANDELAER

Whenever I set eyes on you again, Nivelles,
The day's light fades in measure as you take its place
And memories revive, breathe back to life for me,
Like the dancing of fire in the depths of the bakehouse . . . .
Looking back, I see it all, urchin more wrist than sleeve,
Less gooseberries than prickles, workdays more than Sundays,
Less sunshine than hailstones, but less tears than content
Since I already loved you without knowing it . . . .
And I grew up any-old-how with the riff-raff,
Was a young sprig among the young sprigs of the time
But chief of ragamuffins in our neighbourhood,
Wanting to be one with them, their rare brogue on my lips,
A scrambler up the willows as now I am through life,
Happier looking for nests than looking girls over,
I'd quarrel and call it quits in a moment,
Never dithered in making a fist or a friend,
Pear-scoffer and picker of apples, scrumper of plums,
Sore bowel and bum took a short-cut through my shorts,
With holes in my pockets and out at the elbow,
It was my heart, not ha'pence, made me a richman.

FRANZ DEWANDELAER

Jonquils

Your eyes turned my head
The day we were looking
  For jonquils . . . .

We gathered more kisses in the combs
Than there were flowers to spatter the fields,
More than the glinting of pearls in the pond,
More than the woods cradled jonquils . . . .

A flower well may die but it will not be killed:

And maybe that's why we hadn't picked them . . . .

  The jonquils,
    Upright, golden, scoured, blunted,
Flowers of butter, butter in flower – there were nests of them –
  When we left there were more still . . . .

  You would have liked an armful
  But we couldn't have managed
  Now they blazed in the black firmament –
  Upright,
      golden,
          scoured,
              blunted –
    Star-daffodils . . . .

MAX-ANDRE FRERE

Wood thrown on the grate

The wood that you throw on the grate
to make the fire burn up again
hasn't perhaps the best of fates
but after all there could be worse.

Oh, not the kind of end for me
and yet I'd not refuse the thought
of being wood thrown on the grate
to make the fire burn up again.

Cooking food, keeping out the cold,
and softening the day's fatigues,
isn't that something all the same
well worth the risk of fading out
like the wood that's thrown on the grate.

ALBERT YANDE

El cé qu'est r'voûye

Mâ vôrmè s'i r'vunout l'afant qu'è tcheû d'sa mère
D' dès la bènaye du plètches, su la paye du froumèt,
Qui n'avout pon d'fachète èt qu'an n'savout coumèt
I folout rachandè – el pôeve afant d'mizère . . . .

Lu, pu pôeve quu lès pôeves, qu'est v'nu d'dès les pôeves djans,
Qui n'è yieù qu'in-ètôle pou sa neûtie d'Nowè
Et dès pinsons aus mês – cès mês qu'an d'vout clowè
Pou qu'lès-oumes, du viki, rutrouvinche eune râjan.

S'i r'vunint tout d'in côe cés-la qu'an tchèstout-voûye
Pasqu'il-atint minables, qu'i n'savint doù alè,
Pasqu'i gnavout pèchôene qui s'a v'lout ahalè:
(Toutes lès ôlûches sant bounes, pardiè, quand'an ravoûye . . .)

S'i v'nint r'tchokè à l'uch-èt d'mandé,ne pitite côene
Du pèl, pou z'î mète-bas, pa dlé l'feù qui clârtî,
S'i d'mandint coume d'des l'tès: 'P'lans-dje pasé la neûtîe?'
Pou douvri s'n-uch au lôrdje, gn'arout-m'-t-i co pèchôene?

Dialect of the Gaumais, S.E. Luxembourg province

The Revenant

But anyway, if the child came back that was calved
In a wooden byre, on the straw of the crib,
That had no swaddling cloth and they didn't know
How to keep warm – the poor child of sorrows –

Poorer than the poor, come to live among them
With only a stable in which to spend Christmas
And hands numb with cold – those hands they'd nail up
So that men might find new reason to live:

If they suddenly came who had been sent packing
Because they were shabby and had nowhere to go,
Because there was no-one who wanted to bother
(Any old pretext will do to turn them away . . . .)

If they came knocking and asked for a small corner
Of the hearth, to lie down in the firelight,
If they asked, can we stay the night, as they did once,
Would there still be no-one to throw the door open?

I fasten doors and windows
For fear night force the house;
Into our corners we fold,
Each to himself, like brooding hens.

For all two share the hearth
No word is hasarded;
Hearts sink into the silt,
Isolated, lacerated.

Souls, meaner or heavier,
Flag under the flesh . . . .
I feel the past lag on my skin
Like a scoop of burning cinders.

LOUIS REMACLE

The Dream

My heart was leaping from a dream so good.
When I think of it now there rises deep down
A sharp regret all the colours of my youth . . .
So many girls for me with opened arms
And leave to go as I was welcomed there.
But you, the choice whom I had never met,
What did we do to live so many years
Unrecognized, unseen, on the same earth?
And at the very end to find ourselves
When dreams are dead and days for dreaming past . . .

Happiness

The living star of other days
slipped down from my window.

Shadow, like a heavy fog,
had laid my lids asleep.

Voices there, young voices,
clear voices like young bells,

Rose up and sang to me
all the happiness I'd dreamed of.

And I entered very quietly
the old house with its large doors.

Then of a sudden could no longer hear them
and the walls shone with light.

LOUIS REMACLE

By the castle

I was playing in the sun and you were not near me.
The castle was waiting with its great white walls,
Its little windows, as if it saw coming all the days
Of my childhood on the road across the fields.

Where were you? Wasn't this road unrolling towards you?
The breeze of my summers was dawdling in the beeches;
And as it shifted the shadows about me and the sun
There was no-one to tell me how slowly the hours passed.

Where was I? Wasn't this road on the way towards me?
It pilgrimaged across the sky in long procession;
And on my knees in the grass, unhearing, unseeing,
I was laughing as I looked for beech-mast in the ruts.

I was playing by myself among the castle beeches;
Even had they been shown me, I'd not have recognised
All my feverish days in a twittering flock
That sang like birds on the highest branches.

JEANNE HOUBART-HOUGE

Roads

Roads run at random
and wander over the earth
shutting in the seasons.

Like the pearls of a great necklace
they thread green villages
and towns the colour of smoke.
They would like to reach heaven,
the roads that run at random.

There are too many pearls on their way,
there are too many pearls to thread.

Men walk at random
and wander over the earth
shutting in shadows.

Like the beads of a great rosary
they tell their suffering,
their joys, their pleasures and desires.
They would like to reach heaven,
the men that walk at random.

There are too many beads to their lives,
there are too many beads to tell.

The roads run at random,
men walk them to the end.

But the rim of heaven
rolls back at each step
they take in the dust
of the roads
        that run at random.

Rain-wind

The witch of dead illusions
Beats back and forth through the cold night of griefs
And,
Like the stains that keep reappearing on a Sunday dress,
The mauve cobwebs of a forgotten bereavement
Leave their film
about the garden of last loves.

Pour soul that rises without call,
Boon the devil has granted,
New face already seen to excess!

Is that why the wind comes whispering?

Summer's fiddle

The fading fiddle of summer
Still tries a tune over.
The wordless song and the last green of the trees
cradles the memory of roses.

You'd like to give up your failings, your questions,
to give up human attachment
and think only of green.
A branch,
just a branch that brushes the window,
a branch of green
which turns into something immense,
some immeasurable thing
you do not know how to grasp.

WILLY BAL

White walls

The old, old houses at siesta time,
the old, old good-folk, peacefully dozing,
leaning their heads back in their chairs . . . .

A grey cat naps in an aproned lap,
and the whole household sleeps and dreams of auld lang syne
while the great oak clock softly balances its leads.

White walls on which the harvest sun
shivers, its blade eclipsed, then reappears
sieved through thin blinds and gently spilling over.

The house drowses as if it might be waiting
for someone who went off long ago, whose yellowing
photo in the drawer still makes his mother weep.

The old-folks take their nap; harvesting goes on outside,
but here the perfume of box unleaving slips
from between a prayer-book's thumbed and riffled pages.

Glossily, furniture gleams in the slanting sun,
polished by many hands as though pampered with caresses,
sideboard, cabinet, corner-cupboard.

Three is striking; the house begins to stir . . .
The pot is singing on the stove; coffee-time soon.

Fire!

There was the cottage blazing,
The parson was ringing the bell,
Local copper in a flap,
The mayor swearing blue-murder.

But folks were out after berries and nutting,
Building castles in spain or chasing the girls,
Cheek by jowl in the shop of day-dreams.
The sharpest were gleaning, afraid of losing a grain.
    Step by step they got on with their business
    And it all mounted up by and by.
Mickle and muckle, hand over hand, they laid in,
Sharp fellows; and by way of relaxing
Between two good strokes, they passed on a joke.

    And the world thundered
    Like a skittle-alley floor.
    The world split at the seams
    Like an old bit of rag.

That was surely the neighbour's went up!
When the lot's burned, the fire will go out.
If you want to live quietly, turn a deaf ear.

MARCEL HICTER

The crosses

If they were set out in two rows
all the little storm-chewed crosses
all the little crosses put up in haste
at cross-roads, on hill-tops,
if they were set out in two rows
all the little crosses that no-one looks at now,
all the white crosses, all the brown,
all the little crosses that are all that is left
of a man's youth and heart and pride,
all the white crosses no more than a name
that the rain gnaws and rases week by week,
a lord's name, shopkeeper's, workman's,
name of noble or bastard, father or son,
married, betrothed,
all those little crosses no more than a name
of one or another who died for their world,
mouthing the dust with a cry for freedom
who fell to the soil
their fathers worked so long,
who fell so many weeks away
from homes empty of their laughter,
of the strength of their arm, their joy in living,
so many weeks away on the further side of the world
on a foreign road they knew nothing of,
all these little crosses all that remains
of boys called up from the four horizons
who fought for the same cause,
all these little crosses no more than a date:
May the eighteenth nineteen fourty,
August the twelfth nineteen fourty four,
all these little crosses no more than a name:
JOSEPH DUBOIS   FRANCOIS KINABLE
MARIUS ABADIE   GONZAGUE D'ABLANCOURT
BORIS CHAPOULNIKOV   ALEG PIKUZINSKI

SILBERMANN   SAMUEL LEVY
JOHN F. O'HARA   CHARLIE B. MAXWELL
KOUNDOURIATIDES   LOU TSEU YANG
      MOHAMMED MIMOUNI
all these little crosses of boys from everywhere
fallen for the same cause
who died the most diverse of deaths,
crosses for those struck down from the sky,
crosses for those dragged under,
crosses for those burned alive,
crosses for those with their head full of shot
(like little Gregory in the song),
crosses for those who were blown in pieces
whom no-one in the world could recognise,
crosses for those lead out
with eyes bandaged to the cold of the dawn,

if they were set out in two rows,
the crosses of all the young men who died for us,
they would make an avenue that circled the earth
and embraced every nation,
whatever their colour, whatever belief,
and would bring them together
and would keep them together
and would teach them
love.

JEAN GUILLAUME

Strength

We toss up the hay to the lofts
        by forksful
And tip stooks over on the floor
        straddle-armed,

Glad to be bodies unleashed
        to the wind's lash
And letting it bite without wincing
        or flinching an inch,

Now more than ever we want to be
        strong as the trees,
Knuckling new shapes into the grain
        of every harvest.

One Day

The weather will be calm
and we'll leave unhampered
to encounter summer.

They'll have cleared the dirt
out of the old cart.

And when we ride back down
at nightfall
with our dust-white horses
harnessed to the harvest of children,

the tears come that will tear out our eyes.

43

JEAN GUILLAUME

At table

There was an empty chair at table.
There was a grey pearl's noiseless passage
Down cheeks the fire of tears had scorched.
They'd opened the door to the cellar . . . .

But nobody came up again.
Perhaps it was too late already.
No-one spoke. It was summer.
It was evening. Nothing left in the carts.

Old person

We left her to one side,
She might have been the servant.
And all day we wrung her heart
Which was no more than a rind.

"Plenty of her sort about,"
Was how we put it in passing;
"Two a penny, folk like her.
Drink up, Jack, we're off."

Our eyes were scarcely moist
The day her time was up.
Two tears are enough to wipe off
A name written in chalk.

Too bad for us that art is lost!
There's so much to relearn
Of dying with an air
Of having lived – before the end.

LEON WARNANT

After

After the long black pages
here's a white one for Sunday;
& you shirt-sleeved in the sun
listening to the evening bells.

After six close-written pages
you've reached one to look at,
        with illustrations.

Well, you'll say, tomorrow there'll be more
                long pages,
        enough to give you writer's cramp,

            but what matters
            would be knowing
        when you close the book
    what new one will be given you,

what pages you will find there then,

        & if there'll even be one.

LEON WARNANT

Bad dream

What are you doing at the last ball's entrance
with your good shoes
broken down
with your fine Sunday costume
creased
the cuffs of your blouse left undone
and your neck sticking out like a bird-perch
with your eyes so full of fever
they might be oil-lamps glaring?

In the morning
dew a
red slug in the grass
looks like a pair of lips.

On an air for player-piano

They have trained up hedges
Taller than steeples
So you can't cut a cup
From the walnut wood.

But behind tall hedges
Boys with no playthings
Look up at the walnuts
From under old steeples.

They have leapt the hedges,
Leveled the steeples,
The walnuts are shelled
And the trees cut down.

With wood from the hedges
They build back the steeples,
Put the nuts in the earth
So the trees grow again.

For boys with no playthings
They have planted crosses . . .
The crosses make hedges
But not tall enough.

And back come the cups
And the leveled steeples,
Good folk without pay
And raids on the walnuts.

But, my heart murmurs, under the earth
There isn't a hedge or a frontier,
Only friends at siesta time.

ALBERT MAQUET

Sick man

The man who had eyes in place of his hands and
nothing in place of his eyes lay bedridden till
yesterday.

I brought him a cup of camomile and while I
stirred the sugar with a silver spoon his hands
watched my eyes while his eyes did nothing.

*

What time is left he passes
Watching it grow like a flower,
His hand glued to the window,
His long thief's hand.

The others, huddled by the fire,
Drowse and contract
As their frosting dreams
Freeze to the pane.

Make no noise to wake them,
Be still if you enter.
Hand, flower and window
Are not what you think.

ALBERT MAQUET

The hour

All the cats looked alike, gargoyles in stone
Whose slit lids let escape a gleam of gold.

Wordless, the great trees with upraised arms
Steadied the toppling sky of clustered stars.

It was not the globe of the moon that shone
But all moons at once since the world began.

And everything so hushed all you could hear
Was flit of fireflies in the foliage.

We took our time, walking pressed close in dread
At so much happiness we might drop dead.

ALBERT MAQUET

Stranger

Folk, all the acquaintances I'd had
Would make believe they were dead to cut me.
The others would watch me pass like the plague
From the shelter of their narrow windows.
Wherever I'd be, no-one there but myself.
Nothing hidden but at my approach.
Water, the ponds would rebuff my face
And my shadow itself leave no trace now.
It would be a day that never ended,
As if the darkness flinched back before it.
And so quiet you could hear a fly!
I'd search for a sign to say I existed;
Then feel so alone all at once
I wouldn't know where to go any longer.
I'd stretch out there full length on the stones
And see the sun through my lids.
I should think of nothing. Let myself get well.
Would hear the sound of my blood pumping madly.
And before I needed to come to myself
I'd take my life up, unwrinkled, at will.

MARC DEBURGES

Child

The child lifts day up
spilling light on his face.
He snatches a sunray
and pricks it live into his eye.
Scratches red from the rainbow
to smear it lightly on his cheeks.
The child goes gleaning cobwebs
and makes a silvered headpiece.
He gathers two drops of dew,
a pearl for each ear.
Now he's waiting for nightfall . . .
The child steals a comet's tail
and fashions a collar.
He bites into the moon
and his teeth sparkle like gold.
He takes small handfuls of stars
and sprinkles a royal crown on his head.
Then the child becomes man.
And a man wants all of the sun,
all of the stars,
all the moon,
all the day,
all rainbows.
And, suddenly, he dies.

Departed

They've been hammering all night
at the cartwright's in the village.
Seems like you just can't make
a coffin and no noise.

That upset everyone
except an old-timer asleep
in his black swallowtails
that the barber helped him on with.

NICHOLAS DONNAY

The ultimate party

Believe me, folks,
when my hour comes
to shuffle the cards
the very last time
you'll all be in bed
with your adipose
productive wives,
blissfully unaware,
I know, like the petty
bourgeois that you are . . .

And I, by myself.

Don't worry, however,
I'll shuffle them well,
the dirty cards,
I'll make a good long job of it . . .
till the witches come
astride their brooms
one after another
to squat round the table
and take up the game.

By daybreak the party
will no doubt be over . . .

I shan't be there
to pick up the winnings,
that's all.

It'll be your job, folks,
a task for the middle classes.

JENNY D'INVERNO

Coleûr dè tins

Mi coûr s'anoye, coleûr dè tins,
Coleûr dèl campagne, dès brouheûrs,
Coleûr dè trisse osté qui pleûre,
Gote à gote, âs foyes dès pâquîs.

Èt d'vant mi,li vôye qu'è st-à-sûre
Dizos l'fène plêve qui susinêye,
Rilût tot come ine lâme rid'reût
So l'tchife sins solo dèl vîle tère . . .

Ca l'crouweûr arènih li djôye,
Èt l'sondje qui pîpêye à m'pwètrène
Cwink'sêye sins poleûr s'ènûler,
Neûr èt pèzant come on cwèrbâ.

Dialect of Liège

Weather's colour

My heart flags, the weather's colour,
Colour of fields and mist,
Colour of summer dripping
Tearfully among the box-leaves.

And before me the road I must go
Under the fine rain's whisper
Gleams like a tear that trickles
Down the sunless cheek of the old world . . .

For joy is rusted by drizzle,
And the dream husking in my breast
Rattles powerless to take flight,
Black and brooding, like a crow.

Done for

Old Nick had it coming.
Everyone said so: 'That old,
It's time he died.' They found him
Drowned in his well.

Old Nick had it coming.
He was a torment to himself.
They buried him at eight o'clock;
Two grave-diggers,
Four people at the cemetery.

It was the abbey granger next.
A stout man, strong as a horse.
Died of eating too well.
Small beer!

So, two deaths in a week.
Mass at ten, all of a dither.
Who'll get the oats in now?
The abbey farmer and old Nick . . .
That makes two deaths in a week.

And death comes back and death goes on.
Another oldster gathered in!
It's our neighbour breathed his last.
The dogs howl.

When death starts to husk a village
– Stone knife here, chisels there –
One more trembles, one more struggles
To catch breath . . . . You see nothing else
When death comes to flail a village.

Dji baloujeu mièrnu po rapauji mès fîves
Èt dji strimeu lès nwârs pazias blancs d'nîve.

Èt volà qu'padrî mi dj'oyeu montè doûç'mint
One tchanson qu'lès vikants n'conuchint nin.

A chaque pas qui dji fyeu, lès vwès astint pus fèles.
Li nîve tchèyeut todi, pus blanke, pus bèle.

Èt dji sondjeu qu'mès-ascaujîyes astint trop nwâres
Po fè rawyi lès vikants qu'astint mwârts.

Dialect of Houyet, S.E. Namur province.

GEORGES SMAL

I went out walking on my own to lay my fever,
  The first in the dark byways white with snow.

And heard rise softly there behind me
  A song the living did not know.

At every step I took the voices grew more harsh.
  The snow kept falling, whiter, finer.

And it seemed to me my footprints were too black
  To bring the dead to life again.

Foliage

Foliage beaten down by the wind,
Foliage torn off in the gale,
That drags down the hollow lanes
Behind the dark horse-teams.

One fine day I saw them leaf,
The next I went in mourning;
They would have found more mercy
Under May's caress.

Aghast now, I'm about to pick
The pockets of the hanged.
Sometimes their ropes would dangle
From the foliage of my thoughts.

finished Dec. 27, 1981

AUTHORS

WILLY BAL: b.1916 in the province of Hainaut. Professor at Louvain university. Member of the Académie royale de Langue et de Littérature françaises, and of the 'dialectal academy' – La Société de Langue et de Littérature wallonnes (SLLW). Winner of the Hainaut provincial prize for Walloon literature in 1952 and of the Liège prix biennal for 1954-5. 'White walls' (*Murs blankis*) appeared in his *Oupias d'avri* (April Branches), Editions de La Vie Wallonne, Liège, 1935; and 'Fire!' (*Au feu!*) in *Poques èt Djarnons* (Wounds & Seedlings), Editions du Bourdon, Charleroi, 1957.

GABRIELLE BERNARD: 1893-1963, Namur province. Winner of the national prix biennal, and also that of Liège for 1950-1. 'Cobwebs' (*Filés d'l'Avièrge*) appeared in the collection *Poèmes choisies de Gabrielle Bernard*, La Vie Wallonne, Liège, 1938 – which also contains selections of her French-language work.

HENRI COLLETTE: b.1905, Malmédy, in the northern Ardennes region ceded to Belgium by Germany after World War I. The poem is from his collection *Ploumes du Co* (Cock Plumes), Georges Thone, Liège, 1934.

MARC DEBURGES: b.1922, Hainaut province. 'The child' (*L'èfant*) is from his sole collection, *Tibigôtî* (All and Sundry), 1959.

FRANZ DEWANDELAER: 1909-51, Brabant province. Counted among the foremost Walloon writers. Taken as a prisoner of war, he was repatriated in 1942 in broken health, which he never properly recovered. The poem on Nivelles, his birthplace, appeared in his second collection, *El'Munchat qui crèche* (The Growing Pile), Cahiers Wallons, Namur, 1948; 'Jonquils' (*Les Tchambourées*) is from his 'film poétique', *El'Tchanson du Grisou*, which gained him the Liège prix biennal for 1933-4 but remained unpublished until its inclusion in Jean Guillaume's edition of his *Oeuvres Poétiques*, SLLW, Liège, 1970 (in which the other poem is also to be found).

NICHOLAS DONNAY: b.1926, Liège province. Winner of the Prix des Critiques Wallons for his second collection in 1967 and of the Liège prix biennal for 1968-9 for his third. 'The ultimate party' (*Li dièrinne pårt*) is from his latest collection, *Com on tabeûr* (Like a drum), Imprimerie Smets, Blégny, 1975.

JULES FLABAT: b.1925, Brabant province. President of the local writers' association and editor of their journal, *Nwèr Boton*. His first collection won the Prix des Critiques Wallons (on whose jury he now serves) in 1971, and his second, *Dè blanc sauvion së lès tîlias* (White sand on the flagstones) the Liège poetry book prize in 1974. It is from the latter that 'Departed' (*Evôye*) is taken.

MAX-ANDRE FRERE: 1909-61, Hainaut province. Winner of the Liège prix biennal for 1938-9 with his collection of rondels, *Tchipotrîyes* (Trifles) – published the following year – from which 'Wood thrown on the grate' (*El bos qu'on fout dins l'tukwè*) is taken.

CHARLES GEERTS: b.1900, Hainaut province. Officer of the Order of Leopold II. Literary director of *El Mouchon d'Aunia* (The Siskin), the magazine of Les Scrîveûs du Cente. Winner of many literary medals and awards, including the Prix du Hainaut for his second book of poems in 1952 and the Liège poetry book prize for his third, in 1972. 'Matchstick men' (*Boulomes*) is from his latest collection, *Les-eures d'après* (After-hours), SLLW, Liège, 1978.

EMILE GILLIARD: b.1922, Namur province. Winner of the national prix biennal, and that of Liège for 1958-9. 'Done for' (*Feuwéye*) is from his *Pâters po tote sôte di djins* (Prayers for all sorts of folk), Jean Servais, Namur, 1959.

JEAN GUILLAUME, S.J.: b.1918, Namur province. Professor at Namur university. Member of the SLLW. Winner of the national prix biennal, and that of Liège for 1948-9 with his first collection, *Djusqu'au solia* (As far as the sun), Editions Mosane, Namur, 1947, from which 'Strength' (*Fwace*) is chosen; 'One day' (*On djoû*) and 'Old person' (*Vîye djint*) come from his second, *Grègnes d'awous* (Harvest), from the same publisher, 1949. 'At table' (*A tauve*) first appeared in the anthology *Poèmes wallons* (Paul Gothier, Liège, 1948).

MARCEL HICTER: 1918-79, Liège province. Director-general of the Minstère de la culture française. Winner of the Liège provincial prize. A French-language writer who uses dialect for special effect. 'The Crosses' (*Lès creûs*) appeared in his collection *Gentils gallans de France*, Georges Thone, Liège, 1956.

JEANNE HOUBART-HOUGE: b.1910, Liège province. Teaches Walloon language and literature at Liège. Member of the Liège prix biennal jury and secretary to the jury of the Prix des Critiques Wallons. She won the latter prize in 1957 with her first collection and the Liège poetry book prize with her second in 1960. Her third, *Grîse Teûle* (Grey Cloth), Imprimerie J. Duculot, Gembleux, 1971, from which 'Rainwind' (*Vint d'Lovaye*), 'Roads' (*Vîyes*) and 'Summer's fiddle' (*Li vièrelète di l'osté*) are taken, won the SLLW's silver medal in 1971.

JENNY D'INVERNO: b.1926, Liège. Member of the SLLW and winner of the Prix des Critiques Wallons. 'Weather's colour' (*Couleûr dè tins*) was first anthologised in *Poètes wallons d'aujourd'hui*, Gallimard, Paris, 1961.

EMILE LEMPEREUR: b.1909, Hainaut province. Member of the SLLW; winner of the Hainaut provincial prize, and of the Jules Destrée prize of the Association Royale des Ecrivains Wallons in 1975. His poem appeared in *spites d'âmes: Visâdje* 1934 (*Soul-claps: Face*) in 1935.

GÉO LIBBRECHT: 1891-1976, Hainaut province. After serving all through World War I, he travelled widely and even settled for a while in Brazil before returning to Belgium, where he eventually gave up his avocation as lawyer to take up business. A member of the Académie royale, he was a distinguished poet in French and winner of many literary awards. Of his work in Picard dialect, what is considered best celebrates his native Tournai. One such collection gained him the national Prix biennal de littérature dialectale for 1964. His comic monologue is taken from *M'n accordéion*, Editions l'Audiothèque, Brussels, 1963.

ALBERT MAQUET: b.1922, Liège. Professor at Liège university; member of the SLLW. The untitled poem and 'Sick man' (*Li malâde*) are from his *Jeû d'apèles* (Calling game), Ougrée, 1947; the much anthologised 'Stranger' (*Etrindjîr*) finally appeared in a later collection, *come ine blanke arièsse* (Like a white fishbone), Les Cahiers Wallons, Namur, 1975, as did 'The hour' (*L'Eûre*).

RENE PAINBLANC: b.1908, Hainaut province. Like many earlier dialect writers, a self-taught man of humble origin. A part-time comedian whose prose and drama has won him several prizes, of which the most recent was the 1976Prix du Hainaut for a collection of prose and verse.

LOUIS REMACLE: b.1910, Liège province. Professor at Liège university; member of the Acadamé Royale and of the SLLW. Winner of the Liège prix biennal for 1932-3. 'Happiness' (*Bouneûr*) is from his *A tchêstê d'poûssîre* (Castle of dust), Paul Gothier, Liège, 1946, and 'By the castle' (*Adré l'tchèstê*) in his latest collection, *Mwète Fontinne* (Live source), Les Cahiers Wallons, Namur, 1974. 'The dream' (*Lu sondje*) was first anthologised in *Poèmes Wallons*, Paul Gothier, Liège, 1948.

GEORGES SMAL: b.1928, Namur province. Member of the SLLW; winner of the national prix biennal, and that of Liège for 1956-7 with *Vint d'chwache* (North wind), Les Cahiers Wallons, Liège, 1953, from which both his poems are selected.

JOSEE SPINOSA-MATHOT: b.1921 and brought up in Namur province. Member of the Association Royale des Ecrivains Wallons and several provincial groups. Winner of the Liège prix biennal for 1970-1 as well as several other awards, including the Prix des Critiques Wallons in 1969 with her collection *Feuwèyes* (Flames), Imprimerie Bourtembourg Frères, Nismes, 1972, from which is taken 'On an air for player-piano' (*Su ène aîr dè viole*).

LEON WARNANT: b.1919, Liège province. Professor at Liège university; member of the SLLW. Winner of the Liège prix biennal for 1952-3 with two collections: *Blames èt Foumîres* (Flames and Smoke), Liège, 1953, from which 'After' (*Après*) is taken, and *Lès-annâyes èt les vôyes* (Years and Paths), Liège, 1955, from which comes 'Bad dream' (*Mâva sondje*).

ALBERT YANDE: b.1909 in the Gaume (Belgian Lorraine), Luxembourg province. Honorary director of the provincial government, and a member of the administrative councils of the Luxembourg Archaeological Institute at Arlon and the Musée Gaumais at Virton. Member of the SLLW and the Luxembourg Academy. 'The Revenant' (*El cé qu'est r'voûye*) is from his third collection, *Dokèt d'fènasses* (Bouquet of wild grasses), Michel Frères, Virton, 1966, which gained the Liège poetry book prize the year previously.

FURTHER READING

Several anthologies might serve as samplers of Walloon writing in the original, including *Poèmes Wallons* (Paul Gothier, Liège, 1948), *Anthologie du prix biennal de littérature wallonne*, ed. Octave Servais (Ville de Liège, 1963), and *Littérature dialectale d'aujourd'hui* (SLLW, Liège, 1978). Two others might be found more accessible. *Poètes wallons d'aujourd'hui* (Gallimard, Paris, 1961), edited by Maurice Piron, contains his translations into standard French opposite the original texts, several of which poems also figure in the present anthology. It too is part of the UNESCO Collection of Representative Works. Piron's latest venture, *Anthologie de la Littérature wallonne* (Pierre Mardaga, 37 Rue de la Province, B.4020 Liège, 1979) is by far the most inclusive and the best we are likely to see. This covers writing in all three dialects from the 17th century to the present day, and incorporates explanatory notes or translations, as well as biographical and bibliographical information.

For more specialised reading there is Octave Servais' *Contribution à une esthétique de la poésie wallonne*, and the philological works of Léon Warnant, Louis Remacle and Willy Bal. One might mention in particular Remacle's *Syntaxe du parler de La Gleize*, Bal's *Lexique du parler de Jamioulx*, Flori Deprêtre and Raoul Nopère's *Dictionnaire du wallon du Centre* and Jean Haust's *Dictionnaire Liégeois*. Anyone interested in taking the subject further might apply to the recently opened Bibliothèque de la Pensée wallonne at the Echevinat de la Culture in Mons.

YANN LOVELOCK was born in Birmingham in 1939. He has collaborated in several translations, mostly from Eastern languages, for UNESCO. This, however, is his first solo undertaking and excursion into European literature. Previously he was the editor responsible for the foreign language sections of the Pan-Caribbean anthology *Melanthika*. He is also a widely published poet in his own right, a reviewer of far-ranging interests, and a part-time lecturer in English & American Literature.